Dance In The Cage of My Bones

Luella Kerr

Dance In The Cage Of My Bones

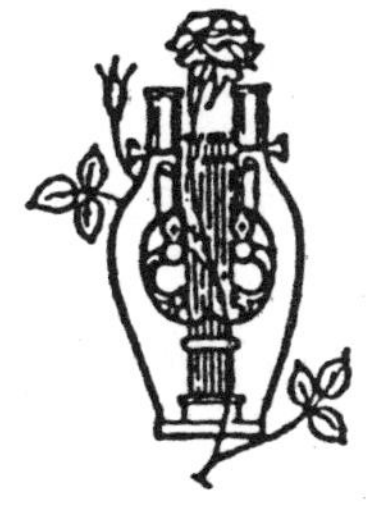

Ekstasis Editions

Canadian Cataloguing in Publications Data

Kerr, Luella
    Dance in the cage of my bones

Poems.
ISBN 0-921215-59-2

1. Breast--Cancer--Poetry. I.Title.
PS8503.067D3   1992   C811'.54   C92-091687-2
PR9199.3.K47D3   1992

© Luella Kerr, 1992
Cover art by Noreen Tomlinson
Frontispiece by Luella Kerr

Published in 1992 by
Ekstasis Editions
Box 8474
Main Postal Station
Victoria, B.C. V8W 3S1

Acknowledgements:

Some of the poems in this book previously appeared in the following magazines: *Quarry, Prairie Fire, Cross-Canada Writers' Quarterly, Arc, Room of One's Own* and *Orbis*.

Dance in the Cage of My Bones has been published with the assistance of the Canada Council.

Contents

Part One
Slipper Shuffle

In My Present Life

Nothing is as it was before.
Seasons occur in their regular order
of course. Trees have sent
ochre and burnt orange notes
as usual, but even after ironing
the fallen leaves,
I am unable to read messages
carried by blotched veins.

Very early in the mornings,
shadows on the wall
create odd calligraphy.
Laughter strikes in the living room.
When I enter, nobody is there,
although hints of autumnal celebrations
lie like jagged metal on the floor.

Silences are shrill,
and the beloved figure whose face
is a scar of dreams so white
their light preceded me,
cannot be found.

Nothing is as it was before.

Bad News

Examining myself, I found a lump the size of a tiny pea in my left breast—and time became important.

Mouth dry, fear crawling up my throat, I phoned my doctor's office. A few days later, the lump examined, my underarm probed, she shook her head: "I don't like it, it's hard. It could be cancer."

An order slip in hand, next morning I had a mammogram, my breasts one at a time flattened like a slab of beef between two plates, the x-ray pictures properly taken.

Dialogue With The Surgeon

"Can't you take off part instead of the whole thing, do a lumpectomy? I have always led an active life. My relationship's important, my man...What about muscles?...A biopsy first?"

"We do that", he said, and handed me my shirt. "Perhaps I won't be able to endure a mastectomy. But I want to do what is right."

His tone was curt, his small hands his lobster and truffles. "I don't take muscles. You'll endure it alright. You can have reconstruction."

He told his secretary to book me a bed, mentioned hospitals were crowded, said I'd probably have a while to wait.

I smile. He smiles, and ushers me out.

Second Opinion

The second surgeon is older, a warmer more solid sort, seemingly unmoved by self-importance. He too says, "mastectomy, your nodes will have to come out." Taking a section around the lump would mutilate my breast, do I really want that?

Confused, in shock, I cry, sitting on the examination table, my breasts and my feelings hanging out.

I ask if he will do the job? No, I am his colleague's patient.

A fine rain falling. Business people scurry, lunch hour on their minds. Others huddle in entranceways. Walking to the bus, I swerve to avoid a lady, her bent head and neck a question mark. The lethal points of her umbrella just miss my face.

That Was A High Day

Does our government give enough
to cancer research? I've sold
daffodils and tags, but this is
small potatoes.

And I don't feel brave.
I am no Terry Fox, no Fonyo,
Canadian heroes running one-legged
across the second largest country
in the world, raising millions.
I saw Steve Fonyo when he dipped
his stump, dumped the vial
of Atlantic water in the Pacific,
the rain lilting, the crowd
uplifted. Oh,
that was a high day.

But now—has the lump grown
this past month? The crazy cells—
have they multiplied? Are they
spreading through my body?

Stranger

Come back,
you refuse to be re-created,
familiar, dear.
The walls breathe you
in and out, the bed
mutters about you,
but I know this is
my tossing and turning.

I remember your hard hat
nodding at me, nodding,
as if it were yesterday.
I was leaning out our fourth
floor window waving,
my fingers wavering,
boneless as fronds.

Now when I need you most
I can't even reach you
by telephone.

Come back

**I forgive everything—
your lies your truth
even nagging, yes**

and I forgive myself
for being older than you are
and loving you so much.

Research

I have ploughed through welters of dull prose on breast cancer:
books, magazines, material by pharmaceutical laboratories.
Findings on new drugs are mixed, treatment varies from region to
region. English reports on lumpectomy claim it effective. Should I
go to Vancouver? To Toronto where I was born? There isn't time
enough for this.

Two big fists thrum my temples, a headache, and my eyes burn.
Library books should go back. Time for that.

Tramping through puddles, my eyes milk the landscape for relief:
rain beaded on plush green; a pair of bulbous miniature cedars
phallic as all-get-out; sturdy rows of corn in a backyard plot. Oh the
earth gives, and my body—tuned by aerobics, steadied by stories my
grandfather told me of courage, pioneering forbears—performing
very well on the edge of fear and hope.

Waiting

Chest X-rays, a cardiogram, reveal no problems, but my physician is grave. She cannot assist the surgeon as she said she would, she's sorry. I am sorriest of all. This stillness gathering behind my eyes is ominous, lonely. Maybe soldiers know, waiting for noise, some sign of the invisible enemy. Or loons. Those solitary birds whose cries sob into the singular dark.

This afternoon the hospital called. Come in anytime before noon tomorrow.

I have crossed to the other side of the world and stand in a field of daisies. I am deaf and blind, my memory also shot away. I lie down with the blue girls of summer, among the innocent flowers, my face turned to the sun.

Everything Fades Away

In hospital, a country crackling with white uniforms and caps, civilians relax in the lobby. Roses and baby's breath arrange themselves prettily in little china boots in the gift shop. A high brown counter protects a computer screen, a head nods, finds my orders. My hand shakes so much, my signature sprawls sloppily on the official Consent to Procedures....

The silver needle gleams like the nurse's morning face, then punctures my hip. Everything fades away. The attendant, the moving trolley...the Operating Room doors, myself...

Another Bad Dream

My surgeon and physician avoid me. Have they gone to another planet? He came prior to operating, stood at the foot of my bed for three minutes. Her face hung over me, a three-quarter moon on a foggy night, once; then blackness swallowed her words and her shape.

Six days have dragged along, six nights, in this sexless world of stiff sheets, hard little glass sticks. The daily ceremony of the thermometer is a highlight in this unfunny play. Serious paraphernalia of the medical arts makes me feel it would be flippant to complain——even when I'm feeling fine, I dislike confrontations.

I wait for the night nurse's rounds and medication. This is another bad dream?

The Volunteer

Her fingers lend authenticity
to the sullen mound
of flesh-coloured foam
supplied by the Cancer Society—
a falsy, drawn
from a drawstring bag.

She tells me she had
breast reconstruction,
has felt fine
the past ten months,
is happy with her paycheque
and her new boyfriend.
I tell her
she looks delicious
in strawberry red,
reassure her when
she pulls her blouse tight:
"I can't tell
which breast is which".

I won't forget her kindness,
or how as she sat,
cheerful traffic,
the music of the streets
came close, was real.

Main Man In My Life

He is back from the bush,
contract completed,
folds into a chair. I
haven't much to say, wish
he would call in a nurse,
speak to a doctor—
to anybody
other than me.

He is like a cat
always lands on his feet,
like cats, prefers to stay
not too involved.

Close-up, his eyes
though, are human
and teared
with sympathy.

Lonely In Hospital Corridors

This whining flesh
this teary blob
humiliates my soul!

Lonely in hospital corridors,
smells stuff my nose,
flowers remind me of funerals,
I long for fresh air.

Tomorrow I will visualize
the bluff at Dallas Road,
a strong Self
graceful as seagulls
and flirty little fishes,
the sun, wind on my skin.

Tomorrow I will visualize
myself whole; today
my right arm
protects my chest,
fragile, foreign
under the hospital gown,
I tremble back to bed.

The Nurse

Eight days after the operation, the surgeon—a small man, disdainful chin, does not like the smell of organized catastrophe—casually says he'll leave an order for one of the nurses to take out the drain in my chest.

Today, the black band on the nurse's white cap leans over my face. She draws the drain out of its tight hole near my breastbone without even a pop. A glass test tube, a quarter inch of gangrenous green in the bottom, swings out of sight. So do her tongs.

I want to kiss the nurse's feet, mark her somehow, set her apart from common mortals. I am so grateful I want——too late, she has taken her crisp efficiency somewhere else. I embrace my relief.

M—M—Arm

My miniature television set
hung on its Marvellous Maneuverable Arm,
revives my juices.

Mornings
I follow as best I can
my aerobics class.
Referring to xeroxed instructions
on post surgery behaviour and exercise,
I obey the hospital plan.

Nights
I search out to shampoos, computers, cars
b & w pictures of dead Hollywood stars
with the urgency of an excommunicated lover.
I am not alone.
A dark shape bends over my bed,
light on the strong square face—
Tarzan—in this alien medical jungle.

Only A Madman Or A Poet

Pink magnolias
stuck in his hatband

hands lost
among a reckless cutting
from his bush

Only a madman or a poet
would strew magnolias
on my pallid sheet,

eyes gleaming
behind thick lenses
make small talk
so quick so pink
figures of dark and terrible gods
seen earlier vanished
and in their place

A plain glass jar of magnolias
petals beginning to brown,
vigorous bushes of the bloom
planted in corners
of the four-bed hospital room.

Slipper Shuffle

Doing my slipper shuffle, I see my former neighbour in a room by herself, lids closed, very pale. Someone has brushed her hair, wisps of white soften her long journey, lines traced on her cheeks, detours taken, asteriks left by laughter at the corner of her lips. There are interesting hollows in the landscape of her face. The very old are often beautiful.

Late afternoon sun warms me, even through drapes. Food on my supper tray, formerly sitting slack and obscene, today has colour and shape. Chrysanthemums in a blue vase funnel the yellow light of Arles.

I begin to think of going home, painting——on my knees on the living room floor—and of my poems, luminous lines, fierce with involvement, zooming out of my head onto the page, with no effort, no effort at all...

Where is my purse on this heaped bed? I did bring a pen.

Please Open The Doors

Hospital wards shut doors,
imprison the mind,
expand irritations already
threatening to explode
the easy rhetoric
of the status quo
through which M.D.'s
strut, godlike.

"Ask your doctor.
You'll have to speak
to the surgeon about that."

Nobody talks of the future,
all lips are sealed.
Sufficient is the day,
routine.

For one's own good,
the body's truth
is contained in neatly
labelled samples—
paper cups of urine
delivered daily to the lab,
ruby rows of small corked bottles,
blood drawn
from reluctant groping veins.

The body's truth retrained,
as if the patient
was a stumbling infant
an unfit amateur
best kept shut away
and uninformed,
and the guards professionals,
bored adults.

Part Two
Out And Around

Anguish

No other word will do
for this gut-wrenching heaving,
the horrible sound coming out.
I am sitting on the toilet lid,
taps running, door locked,
my nightie scrunched
in my hands, damp spreading.
The tears won't stop.

I could not bear him
to see my blotched face,
eyes pinched shut,
mouth ugly, strained open.

Or the gross lopsided torso.
Never in this raw light.

Out

Now I tell you Fall on your knees
                    Gwendolyn MacEwen

My hands, white mice
quiescent on the wheel,
steer my baulky car
through October-smoky air,
the City's shadow-making light.

Hungers, lively wants
the orange gourd of a moon alone
cannot satisfy, flicker
like a bonfire. I taste
freedom.

Taste again in the house
decorated for Hallowe'en,
the Women's Network dinner,
first time socially out
after my mastectomy.
When I set down
my pineapple upsidedown cake,
the hard falsy slips. Unashamed,
I finger the thing back
into place. "Red wine
or white?" the president
tucks a cushion at my back.

Sometimes only a same gender group
can make magic, restore
confidence. Fall on my knees,
healing has begun.

Christmas Shopping

Poking through the mall
for just the right gifts to take south,
I am astonished
when carols stop, iron grills
are pulled across shops. Outside,

ghosts of past Decembers,
whirl under parking lot lights,
wind smacks my cheeks.
I have missed deep snow in the east,
the snap and crackle of winter.

Wool toque to my eyes,
comically loaded with boxes and bags,
I would lie down
if I could, make a snow angel,
blizzards do not last long.
Life reasserts itself,
losses dwindle,
like snow in the Kalifornia of Kanada.

People hunch, stand stiffly,
in the shelter a cough is embarrassed.
Have we become
overzealous guarding privacy?
Each individually wrapped in a life?
When headlights cone
the flowing curtain of white
I want to shout:
"Merry Christmas! Here comes our bus!"
Shyness freezes my voice.

Little Girls

Little girls with greedy legs
munch air all the way
from my house to the store, lost boys
following, thin as snow falling. Ho!
to the day's wit, all messages
from sturdy sources. The trussed park
at road's turning, ice
beading trees, the sun
a Rabelaisian bear, lumbering
my bones bright, my blood's
provisioner.

Chores

The sun
her rays a giant broom,
has swept up
the final traces
of sudden snow.

The Wedding Dress

Animated dolls
two schoolgirls redo their eyes,
hide moist exciting pictures
of holiday parties, boys,
under pink and violet shadows.

My secret is packed,
the bride's dress, off a rack,
white lace top, navy blue
ballerina skirt. And white pumps.

I wanted Juliet sleeves,
big puffs at the shoulders,
seed pearls, a matching headpiece.
When my groom-to-be was out
I'd groan and sew, sew and groan,
alternately cursing surgical cuts
and cooing over my work.

The girls leave, taking their giggles
and whispers. The Ladies Room
is a porcelain tomb. Is the bench stone?
Who is that in the mirror?
She looks like an escapee
from Dante's Inferno!
Blusher helps, I try a dance step.
No ginger in this weary Rogers
and where is my Fred Astaire?

Las Vegas coming up.
The wedding chapel, the lights.

Layover

A bus crunches ice,
spits out three parkaed men.
No sign of him, only a pause, then
one rotund lady in furs
lowers herself onto snow,
pushes her bulk defiantly forward
against the wind.

All this glass is offensive.
Glass doors, closed,
the long stretch of windows,
nothing outside the airport, whiteness
glaring on glass.
Nobody to come in,
people derelict lounges, open dark shops.

He has taken his face,
a flap opening, shutting
words dropping on me like paste,
into Kansas City. Speechless,
I had to lie down.

He is sitting in the chair,
barber's cape flourishing away,
cheeks patted, ruddy, admiring himself.
He may have mentioned a haircut.
My watch is a smirk on my wrist.

And I had begun to think *we*, not
a clumsy cementing of disparate objects
nothing like that, no old couple
features grown identical
perhaps resembling their elderly dog:

a recognition,
at the very least the perception
that he and she
had arrived in the same country,
barriers down, seasons intertwined.

Las Vegas Is

Chill wind at the quiet end of the strip
taking my breath away, moving closer
at a stop the bus might have forgotten.

Three miles of icy brilliance—
so many signs glittering,
hotels, casinos, such a fury of colour—
my breath catches again in my throat.

Waiting our turn, stiff as shy kids,
in soft ivory light of the Registry Office,
our nervousness finally dignified
when a grey-haired cherub clerk
hands us our *Marriage Licence.*

Elephants onstage.
Barebreasted show girls in towering headware.
An unbelievably inexpensive bottle of champagne.
Riding back to our hotel
in a taxicab spacious as a limousine.

Las Vegas is three layers of tulle
floating back from my face,
swirling around lacey shoulders
in The Little Church of The West.
It is really to see one another for the first time,
flawless, every imperfection erased
because each fault is beloved.

His smile, my luminous sun.

Dade City

1.
It's 92° Fahrenheit. The playground looks too tired to support grass.
Trees drip moss, I drip sweat, can hardly sit. Long sleeves suffocate,
but my arm is swollen twice normal size.

Two days ago, landing in Tampa after midnight, my large piece of
luggage was located, ripped, my metal carrier lost. Embarrassed at
causing delay, I entered the house after the long drive, exhausted,
admired the blue cake, foolishly rested my weight on the nearest
clear space, a small table which gave way. I fell hard—under the
floor covering, cement.

2.
Disney World, the Catholic Church are emphatic musts. Driving
through miles of flat rural land, we stop to snap pictures. Branches,
oranges grow from my head. *I want to lie down, rest.* My hip bones
scream in silent unison with all the rest of me. Astounding white
sand seen briefly at a beach, towering nude tree trunks, their absurd
green heads, doing dishes, move along the pain-filled stupor of air-
conditioned days. Nights, the fan creaks with my second thoughts.

3.
Visit insistently requested, his air fare paid, the lone male hauls
heavy trash in the backyard, bags leaves, undisturbed by his sister's
orders, turgid heat. At this point, I do not know how opposites can
possibly attract. I'm a water person, grew up in Toronto near Lake
Ontario, summered on the family island, *Crete*, in Muskoka.
Within walking distance of the ocean the past seven years, I'm
certain now I will never live landlocked.

4.

Christmas Eve, the air cooler, my in-laws more relaxed, we walk to
a street aptly named, churches on both sides, curbs aflame with
candles, stop where the massive floodlit antebellum facade of a
church rears behind a stage, rows of metal chairs on the lawns.
Mother and son move down the aisle, she chooses from empty
rows, beckons. I am anxious, reduced, a suddenly wary animal on
the periphery of the family reunion. If only I had a rubber ring to sit
on. "What is the program, how long? Are we early?" My
bridegroom nods yes, smiles vaguely from behind his mother's
back, sits where she points. I excuse myself.

Around the corner, I find three plank walls raised in someone's
front yard, straw raked over grass——a Nativity tableau. A young
Joseph, beard askew, a sweet-faced girl lulling her Baby Jesus doll, a
donkey with brown-pansy eyes patiently standing. And I thought I
was losing the small light we carry within us, faith, hope, call it
what you like, the divine in the world that carries us forward day
after day...

In ballooning dark, maroon robes of a choir fade in and out. Years
ago I cracked my sacrum, from the feel of my tailbone pressed to
metal, I did it again when I fell... There is nothing creative about
pain... One carol's refrain, sung in a clear soprano, startles me back
from my reverie. I recognize my new niece.

Waiting for the girl, my Music Conservatory years won't be denied.
I look to the red-haired mother and uncle, turn to the white-haired
widow who dominates each scene—"Maybe piano lessons now and
later train her voice...? It's true and big for her age..." Nobody
answers. Maybe nobody heard.

On the walk back I don't try to keep up.
Before year's end, New York, my silent litany.

High On Manhattan

on my handsome youngest son,
little White Plains wife
her New York twang, hugs,
I stagger in pink euphoria
along 23rd, up 7th Avenue's
near frantic jubilance—

>   people massed at corners
>   platoons of taxies, surge forward,
>   halt, move again;
>
>   a man on the run bites into a hot dog,
>   wipes mustard from his mustache;
>
>   the wheeling sun, somewhere above
>   vertical miles of structural
>   steel and mortar, touches
>   a woman's briefcase.

Lost pieces of myself return,
I gulp vibrant air,
my third eyelid lifts:

>   between shafts, men
>   pull carts, push garment racks
>   downwind of traffic, cars
>   carefully elude them.

I get on a bus—the driver chatty
doing a Formula I—get off,
dance in the cage of my bones
down 5th, collapse, chanting *daimoku*
on a bench outside Central Park,

a witness to birds, birds
swooping down from elegant buildings,
sepia soft over the street.

New York Cuisine

Not a fig for fare
in Little Italy or Soho,
not pence for Midtown's bubbling
New Year's brunch—
compared with my son's chefery.
When he presents
the pair of savoury ducks
wreathed in watercress
his hazel eyes thaw my heart,
flash-frozen by medical prognosis.

Those wild bells that pealed
the Old Year out, the New Year in
a hundred years ago, immutable,
black and white in my schoolbook,
chime now in my moving blood.

Dipping fresh strawberries
from baked Alaska's vanilla depths,
I tell of *Miracle Plays*,
of 12th century English folk
acting out finding berries
growing in winter snow.

My second husband, newly wed, my son
by my first, my daughter-in-law
like each other. Over four
days and three nights of perfect holiday,
we have become a family.
I am filled to the brim with love.

Crows Are Not Very Nice

Stepping out of my car uptown, a double row of oddly quiet crows, ochre claws gripping telephone wires, stare at me. Their eyes are like nails.

Walking, back turned, sudden loud flapping jerks me around. Two birds, rapacious beaks open, fly at my head. Wildly I swing my purse, beat at wings strobing the sun.

Comfortable in my old blue robe, my thinking music—a recording of Glenn Gould in the background—I run the day's events through my mind and find a frightened middle-aged woman, dark hair in a jumble, skirt hiked to her knees, looking back over her shoulder, at the entrance to the medical building.

Did instinct to protect a hidden nest, just plain badness or chemical imbalance in the birds' brains cause the crow attack this afternoon?

I really doesn't matter, from acting in that Hitchcockian scene, I learned I can still run.

News From Toronto

For Ann Jilian

You portrayed Mae West in a movie, the male's dream
long before Monroe
of cushiony salvation—
songs, quips, suggestive hips—
wearing plumed hats, long hourglass gowns,
your cleavage prominent.

No wonder the clipping sent by my oldest son,
your husband's article
were stones on my tongue,
another added, both breasts shorn,
to our sisterhood.
By what sinister accident beyond our knowing?
Mutilated millions on this continent—
a silence of centuries
and our dead unsung.

Tonight on the television screen
you play yourself,
reenact your cancer experience*,
adding to our slight history
speak the unspeakable. At the movie's end
in a red dress, spotlighted on a Vegas stage,
applause a joyous crescendo, you bow,
and smile and smile—

And the Poem which refused to be written
is realized,
lyrical affirmation of all that we are.

The Ann Jillian Story was shown on CHEK T.V. 1989.

Partner

Some men, tactful articles warn, cannot bring themselves to look at or touch, changed and suddenly finite flesh. Some leave. This fact has frozen in my gut.

With first look, my doctor purses lips. "Bad luck, but you are still here." I am glad of that. At home, I stare at small-breasted cover girls, nubile breasts peeking coyly out of underwear. I should have had breasts the size of half an orange, easy to lop! I hate myself, but at the oncologist's office, his remark, two fingers held against my remaining breast——"It's certainly large enough"——pierces to my heart.

On the plus side, my hair has not fallen out from chemotherapy, and my partner seems as eager to 'do it' as ever. He comes into the living room, copper hair wild, naked but for my silk paisley square, his droll penis flip-flopping through green fringe. His Primitive Man's mating dance makes us laugh. Surely shared humour is a bond beyond betrayal?

I take back what I said, he is more dog than cat. No, not that either. There have been nights he slept, satisfied after sex, and I beside him dry-eyed in the dark, obliged to lie only on my back, remembering how I rode him, a horse, supporting my weight on my arms, breasts-swinging, hair untied.

It Should Shoot Like A Star

The second floor waiting room in the cancer clinic is something like a bus terminal. Every so often someone leaves, someone else comes in. We are on a journey, we just don't know our destination beyond the examination cubicle, the hospital gown which has a wrinkled defeated look. Who will be told: Go home, be happy, you are clear of cancer? You don't need to come back to the clinic next week, next month, no, not for a year. Never? I check my card, my number, the time allocated for my appointment, again. I have been waiting for forty-two minutes. The smiley nurse comes to the entranceway. Its got to be my turn—it is, she calls my name.

The oncologist assigned to my case puts on his white-coat voice—"I know nothing about your lung. Ask the surgeon about that, and get him to aspirate your arm: Fine. This man uses a four inch spike, big hand, big body mass, relentless pushing-ivory fluid rises slowly, one millimetre, another, in the plastic syringe. *Squish.* An inch of lymph in the basin, my white blood cells running around in a sewer. I need every single one of them to fight....

A lab technician probes with the needle. "You don't have a good vein." She could sever my arm, leave me a stump!, she reties the rubber tubing so tightly. Finally, the needle slides in, lengthways, buries itself in a vein in the back of my hand. "I'll be back", she says, leaving me——squeamish, attached to plastic tubing, the glass jar. I cannot look anymore.

Blood seeps, Dark rich ruby red.
It should shoot like a star.

No Royal Jubilee

I cannot believe my ears——the oncologist is whining. "Ask your doctor to recommend a therapist, fibrosis can't always be avoided." Tap tap tap tap on my back. He avoids touching the iron bars where I used to have an armpit. Long cool fingers push into my belly, low down. "Mmhuh. You can put your clothes back on now."

When will it all end...? The fingering, fastidious nudging, judicious pinching, prodding of my breast? Obscene——oh——but the decisions made with merely one glance: "Reconstruction is not possible, and I wouldn't touch that for repairs".

I cannot believe my eyes. "I'll ask the questions—you answer!" This chest and thoracic specialist swivels at his desk, turns his back, chats into his dictaphone. From across the room, straining, I pick up a few phrases in the medicalese, and learn that yes, my rib *is* "disengaged".

The Saleslady In The Bay

No form——opague jellied plastic in a cotton pouch, is quite my shape. The simulated nipple is large, placed differently than my own. Behind the damp greyness of my mirrored face, the saleslady coaxes——"See? You look fine." The false breast is definitely bigger than my own right. There is no inbetween.

"$275 for the prosthesis and two bras, $26 each". My smile teeters, slips. The saleslady must have noticed my wince. "I'll put it aside with your name on the box. No problem." Affection——she is so *kind*——moistens my eyes.

Alone, I hide in the airless little room, not wanting to see other women in the lingerie department buying low-cut nylon, silk and lace. Ten minutes later, I sidle to the escalator, ride the silver snake to the main floor.

I am safe among the shoppers, clothed, anonymous, and not entirely sure I'm sane.

Easter Sunday, St. Andrew's Cathedral

My grandfather, a Protestant clergyman, preached hell-fire and damnation, but the God of the Kerrs was benevolent. When I was little I knew when I'd been bad. I meant it when I said I'm sorry, shook in my skin——I so wanted to be good. Head down, I would accept my punishment, first a stern admonition, second a hug.

Clouds of incense boil greyly into air cloistered by stained-window glass. Above the bishop's mitred hat, the crucifix gleams. The circling dance of priests and altar boys is followed by a drone——the bulging auditorium answering the priest.

I stand, sit and kneel imitating my partner. His mother phoned from Florida, insisted I get him to Mass. I peer at votive candles, plaster casts of saints.

Half familiar words fly from my lips like doves. I do heartily repent my sins, the known and the unknown. *God, if I lie, cut off my hands but leave my one breast. I didn't mean to do it. Get cancer.*

Annual Victoria Peace March

Peace pennants, banners, umbrellas
crowd the City Square,
move slowly onto the cordoned street.
Edges of buildings are soft,
some trick of light folds window glass
into bolts of shimmering silk.

Rain slows,
falls like a blessing on our parade,
pokey with children and dogs,
awhir with a wheelchair. We are a Monet*
our colours defeat grey skies.
The red and white of the *Maple Leaf*,
emblems of other nations, rise triumphant
above wet April lawns of the legislature
where pale gulls glide and swoop.

Chestnut blossoms, vines, wreathe heads.
Decorated faces bloom and sway.
Smiles flash to everywhere.
When rain stops, hoots and hands
encore bands, signs bounce to the music's beat,
speechmakers solemnize the microphones.

The air is tremulous with change.

**The Rue Montorgueil Decked with Flags*
            by Claude-Oscar Monet

Part Three
Death Shall Have No Dominion

Research II

Globular light patinas my hands, fingers pulling dough, heels of palms pressing in, turning the ball, kneading until it is elastic, one hundred times. Turn on my heel like my grandmother did, flour smudging her nose, sea blue eyes like my father, with a flourish, butter the pan.

Skills handed down through generations are real enough, and blunt research facts on breast cancer. Someone dies every four minutes somewhere, oh, I am fed up with taboos, metaphors of disaster. The other day some politician on television likened the budget to "a cancer on society". How many good words deep in the bone are lost?

Death shall have no dominion in my kitchenette, at my typewriter I shall be Queen. Ah, the rich yeasty smell of the loaf in the oven, the warm taste of freshbaked bread in my mouth: poetry.

Other Worlds, Other Relationships

My physician brings her voice down
like an axe. "You will have to move on,
find another doctor."

I have come to the mothering ocean.
Cedar logs, smoothed by waves
and rolled onto the beach,
one three feet in diameter,
provide my faded-pink comfortable seat.

Teeming with life, the ocean is wise
beyond belief, her language God's music.
A superb belly-dancer, the setting sun
swirls orange and magenta veils
to the ocean's sinuous beat.

Always an easy patient, complications
may have thrown my doctor. Ah well,
a Galileo of the cancer cell,
a researcher, pockets of his mind
lined with history,
peering curiously through a microscope
at the cell's erratic dance,
might remain forever interested.

Violet dusk deepens. The night sky
is fervent with stars. *Stars.*
Other worlds, other relationships.

Radiation

The olive drab snout of the enormous metal box of a machine almost touches my blue crayoned chest. Take me, monster, I am yours.

For you, ugly, soundless as stone, for your Cobalt breath, I come week after week, smile neat, strip and lie down. Taped at ankles and wrists to the table, I strain to open myself, each pore in my frightened skin.

Can there be healing in this rape? Silence broods in the large room.

The Hots

Alas, these 'hots' have nothing to do with sex or handsome men. They don't flash, they're deep, stay for lengthy periods. Unnatural internal heat burns past coils, smush, the pump, muscles, bones, turns my skin into a clammy blanket.

I sneak into restaurants, offices, afraid a sudden peony-red flood in my face will swivel heads. I feel helpless. Wads of kleenex, fans, can't correct severe menopausal reactions, one of several nasty side-effects of adjuvant chemotherapy.

Disturbed

Getting through each day uses me up. Yet I have frightened myself and my lover, shouting so loudly, in such a red rage, he worried: "You will get us evicted if you keep this up." Blood swelling behind my eyes, energy into my legs—so powerful—my chair hit the wall when I jumped up. To get *at* him. My senses so acute I could see veins branched on his eyeballs.

"Bugger—macho sow—I'm a person for godssake not a mutilated skin sack—you and the fucking doctors—assholes—go to hell—rot!"

He had to grab my wrists. My right arm flailed like a windmill.

Over a triviality. He shovelled from the casserole, the salad bowl, spilled on his placemat.

He could have left me for that.

Red Roses

Two green-collar buds,
petals folded, ruminate.
No alien thorns
on these two cultivated
stems. Nothing
to prick the fingers,
draw blood from the day.

How odd a parody of sex
is full-blown rage,
the frantic breathings,
the flush, groans. Serenity
a far blue country out of reach,
we work toward climax
using words. Violate
the rosy air,
chop it into shards.

Such glittering recriminations!

The roses in their crystal vase
do not shed their dignity.
Their lips are tight.
It is just as well
they know nothing
of yesterday's quarrel. This pair
has lived a smooth life
from nursery to flower shop.

Did their green arms tremble
when I took the card they held?
Sweetheart, his bold printing,
American Beauty red.

Luella At The Chopping Board

Frustrations have sharp teeth
bite into days and nights, chew on my nerves.

Authorities refuse to release vital information,
I would have to sue for copies of medical files
spin my hair into gold, become Rapunzel to pay.

A brutish world, we all know that.
Luella at the chopping board, perplexed
part of the puzzle, humanness, our habits,
feeding for instance,
our silly rules, resentments o canada.

My foot is cold, a slipper lost
somewhere in the laundry perhaps.
Seeds squirt
the honed blade of the butcher knife
drips watery red, *plop,*
the oozy mess slides into the chili pot.

I am appalled at what I have done
to defenceless tomatoes
uncomplaining onions
in the name of Holy Appetite—but I go further
clapping the lid on the steel machine
sealing myths, the mysteries of energy.

We are all beautiful and mean well.
Ground meat like ground dreams
in an hour or so, transformed.

Anger

I did not puncture my own lung.
I did not core a pit in my chest.
I did not render my left arm, my side, useless.
I did not damage my heart.
I did not over-radiate myself.
I did not turn my torso into a disgrace.
I did nothing. Nothing. It is all an accident.

The Report

Called often to Court in defence
of the medical establishment,
the Vancouver doctor's tone is flat,
the bulk of his expensive report,
news to me.

Having examined the patient
and the materials, he advises
my lawyer not to go on, make claims.

He states fluid has collected
under surgical flaps, he gives
his caliper measurement of the pit
in her chest. The hospital records
say—routine. He concurs.

Since the doctors did not pursue
the disengaged ribs after surgery—
he lacks the thoracic specialist's
findings—he concurs.

That while there was some concern
at Cancer Control that this
abnormal chestwall might be
related to her radiation, but since
radiation-induced necrosis of ribs
is exceedingly uncommon, he concurs.
Breast cancer has metastisized.
He concurs with oncologists,
the man on the street, the store clerk,
concurs with everybody. Except me.

I do not believe it. I *will* not.

Grey Rain Has Begun To Fall

Large white pots, flowers and herbs
sit unchanged on my balcony.
Deep pink and red balls of bloom,
geraniums, mums pushed up beside them
beginning to bud, are serene.
Parsley, tarragon and chives,
cut back by use, sprout again.

Above the squat apartment building
next door, a few golden ornaments
hung by a faded sun, glisten
on the massed green of elms.

The report sits again on my lap.
The earth does not heave or split.
Grey rain has begun to fall,
not unusual in October.

Letters In My Cookbook

I keep the letter Aunt Miriam wrote when my mother died in my best cookbook, now out of print. Summers in Muskoka, winters in town, her kitchen was aromatic, her cookie tins filled. She charmed me in an apron over slacks, a couturier dress and Paris perfume. "Not too much fiction" she told me, "read biographies, girl." Today, when my oldest son called from Toronto, regrets squeezed. I did not write and phone often enough. She is gone.

My mother's handwritten note, typed pepper relish recipe, are faintly spotted from splattering sauce. I take them from the book, smooth the ivory paper beginning to tear at the folds, recall as I stir, the lilt in her voice, her pillowing softness—when I scraped a knee, when the redhaired boy I liked, snubbed me in the schoolyard.

Was my mother ever sorry she was born? I doubt it, she would think me a traitor. She was feisty, lyrically Irish, Momma, flat on her back in St. Margaret's, tossing her head, making eyes at the Chaplain, just days before she died.

Tulips

Every-which-way
tulips,
leaves spread,
sagging lips open,
wrinkled stamens exposed;

this one on my right
slumped in the clay vase,
ignoring a fallen petal,
a terrible gap.

A few days ago
they refused to bend
under my admiration,
stood blushing
on slender stems
lips closed,
leaves upright spears
protecting their inner parts.

Now look at them—
they don't give a damn
what anybody thinks
of their vulgar poses—
two at the front
lolled back
laughing at a joke!

When I know
my days are numbered,
will I be as brave
as cut flowers?

Dress Code

Chinatown's neon flaunts autumn roses
in the sky. Trees,
naked on Government Street,
wear diamonds in their hair.
Two hookers in buns-high skirts,
fur bunched under shoulder bags,
loom, as I turn the corner at Broad,
their made-up faces invitations
thrust toward cars.

Do the lights, the trees, whores
think me a snoop? I don't know
why I walk sexy streets
after dark, not even a dog
snuffling leaves at my side.
Colours haunt me, startle,
stop me in my tracks.

Some ancestral wisdom in my genes
impels me forward, a thin long scream.
Could two wet spots on my cheeks
be snowflakes? Is death white?

Some vague sense of nature's fidelity
anticipates spring, the burgeoning—
buds bristling,
shoots breaking the earth—
colours patches in the crazy quilt
I wear, green.

There Are Moments

There are moments
that circle the close blue,
leap like salmon,
slow-drift with gulls,
soundings of the Pacific
below cliffs of granite.

Luminous moments
caught by the mind's camera—
here, now, three arbutus trees,
a small family, strongly
rooted at the edge
of tidal flats.

Part Four
Nothing Is Ever Lost

Alberti's Bulls and Angels

The storm has brought
another poet's rage and mourning,
his bulls and angels
into my rooms.

Despair tangling their hair,
angels hover in corners.
On his knees in astonished dust
Alberti's baffled bull
observes the cape dance,
his blood jet. And all the while
wind crashes through trees,
rams rain against windows.

The wind has crept back across
the Strait. Angels have returned
to Alberti's black and white arena—
the book in my lap
spills light from indigo pigeons,
Andalusian flowers, the eyes
of a woman into which the poet swam
for love; a gentler death
than bullrings know,
soft as air
now the sky has cleared.

In Her Dreams She Speaks To Her Lover

1

Long ago
I stopped being jealous
of naked women you watch in dreams,
your eyes licking
their young flesh.

Why don't you look at me
as if I were an ice cream cone,
instead of grazing my shoulder
your lips absent-minded,
a case book or papers
in your lap?

I did not build thick glass
between us. I've battered
and pounded—not even
one crack.

If only you would turn your head,
look, you would see
I have signed you on the wall
with my blood.

2

Sitting at the table
you fork food,
wear your absence
like a uniform.

How about meat ball medals,
decorations of raspberry mousse?

Diagrams, designs,
tiny pinions and gears
fatten your brain.
You do algebra,
calculate angles of funnels,
curves on plastic moulds.

Silence is hard to swallow and,
Edison in reverse,
you leave me in the dark.

You open your mouth
I lean forward intent,
surprised again. Freckles
that march across
your shoulders have not yet
reached your face.

This stuff's alright, you say,
spooning the dessert.
Why is it pink?

What if I couldn't cook
or you had no stomach?
I would have to invent
a new language—
and invention, you think,
is your province.

                3
I have opened the drapes.
Moonlit waves of your back,
your buttocks,
flow gently toward me.

I am a beach. I receive you
gravely.

I stroke, you turn...
Sometimes we are ordinary,
a slightly faded couple
in a photograph.

Someimes we are a coast of anthems,
beautiful and strong.

4

You lie on the bed
like springtime,
your face
pale blossomings,
your hair
a bronze flowering.

At hyacinth dawn
you sing an Eden song.

I don't want you
to waken yet and hear
the big old crows cawing,
see their dark presentiments
pecking at our garden,
at our pulsing heart
I have hung alongside hearts
of other lovers,

on the tree
that bends its leafy
fruit-rich branches down
within our reach.

Orthmolecular

"Nourishing," my mother would say of food she was currently
pushing—we've all heard it—"Eat your peas, they're nourishing.
Drink that milk, it's good for your bones," or, on the other hand,
"No candy until Sunday".

Modest holder of many degrees, this tall man's books on diet and
megavitamins impressed me. Behind his calm face, arthritics,
schizophrenics, parents of children stricken with cancer, the
desperate and the curious, rest. Some indefinable quality he has
reminds me of childhood and my mother's chicken barley soup.

Orthomolecular treatment is comparatively new, mega-doses of
vitamins too often more suspect than remedies charlatans sold
watered whiskey, sugar pills—from the backs of covered wagons
when the West was young. It took cajolery to get a referral to this
specialist. Isn't any well-lit avenue to health worth travel?

On The Third Day of January

New Year's Eve arrived,
and went, to modest celebrations.
Christmas decorations packed,
only a red poinsettia plant,
straggles of tinsel and pine needles
mention the holiday season.

Five days of welcome snow
have given way to fog. Trees huddle,
mass their dark on a lowering sky,
and drip. Rain pools on the balcony.
The air is dank and close.

O God of clocks and elephants
whose memories supposedly are long,
I cannot forget surgery,
my useless shoulder blade, my arm.
Ribs on the left side of my chest
bereaved of flesh,
my left breast also gone.

Resolutions lie comatose, hymns
wait for winds of change and chance,
the signatures of hope.
I look outside again, and see
against the tenebrous backdrop
of sky and rock, two gulls
flying ribbons of light
above the clearing in the park.

Golden Yesterdays

Not one stick of furniture
looks right. Two days after moving,
unpacked boxes stifle the living room,
the linen cupboard is a mess.

I have left bits and pieces of myself
all over the place,
each move an uprooting,
the same dull sense of loss.

At dusk, I spread peat moss,
puddle and tamp small plants.
Boxes attached to the railing
will breathe colour, loose scent
come summer, my small balcony
will wear a Mediterranean smile.
Now, branches dribble,
the light is heavy, purple.

Trowelling topsoil,
I dig into memory, seeking images
not in photo albums shoved on a shelf.

The Sunday child,
navy reefer brass-buttoned,
velour hatbrim turned up,
small face an attraction of light,
singing her heart out
"Just as I am, O Lord, I come."

Or this woman, two years divorced
wedged in the carrel,
winter boots, coat, her purse
slovenly on the floor,
selecting from tidy stacks
of books on the table
Sir Walter Raleigh's poems.
She thinks of him
locked in the Tower of London,
the bruised dank stone,
in the courtyard below
the neck block in place,
the shining blade sharpened.
Raleigh knew love's alphabet,
knew about time,
"who in the dark and silent grave...
Shuts up the storye of our days."

My knees ache,
my mouth is filled with grit, rain,
golden yesterdays.

Nothing Is Ever Lost

Last night
the bedroom redefined quiet;
mind plumped, I fell asleep
counting Wordsworth's daffodils.
Tonight? Brambles,
a bed of thorns,
my thoughts enraged bees,
without nectar.

My last Will and Testament...
Who wants a 1977 Pacer wagon,
vandalized? My Dodge Colt
a used-car-lot bargain?
The grisly details of survival,
the grislier details of death—
a casket or cremation? So many losses,
it seems, so few gains.
I should go to sleep. Sleep.
Life is not a balance sheet.

My crystal chandelier, heavy
for its size, carried
from house to apartments,
across the country in a plane
grows dust in a friend's attic.
When clean, a silvery sparkling,
a fantasm of lights. Things.
Reminders of what was.
The sofa, loveseat,
worn yet comfortable, lamps.
Reminders of what is.

I give, devise and bequeath
to you whom I love,
stillness, at the still centre
of being, dark and light,
the beauty in the ugly,
more laughter than tears,
the great rushing that is ecstacy...

and the dependable
constancy of change:
magnificent autumn reds,
chartreuse buds in spring,
summer peonies
a burst of fireworks.

And language of course,
uniquely your own, like eyes,
hair, breathing skin.
Take what you like of my poems,
any drawing, oil on canvas,
snapshot albums marked
with your names, don't fight,
remember I love you...
Why cannot I sleep?

On the far wall, a painting,
colours I know by heart,
Butterfly In Flight to that far blue
that draws all light together.
In one brilliant flash
we both will be gone—
o carnal enigma! He,
marblefaced, mouth open,
has rolled onto his back, snores,
pompous, passionless,
a lecture on how to go to sleep
in sixty seconds. Soft
as the stick of moonbeam
sliding between drapes
that don't quite meet. I prod:
"Turn on your side, honeybuns",
and snuggle in.

Nothing is ever lost
that cannot be found,
in some shape or other,
or sensed.

Angels in Windbreakers

Angels in windbreakers
throw balsa darts.
Sleeves move up and down,
white, then blue, feathered
by sun and leafy shadows.

The angels pivot, watch
gliders loop-the-loop;
feet scarcely touching the ground,
they run, leap—
wings out, up—
catch the wood V's
before they hit the grass.

Relaxed in the rattan chair
on the balcony,
paper on my lap,
my hands a *mudra*, I note

how supple limbs,
the slender voices of young boys,
lend themselves to poetry.

Sailing on the Elwha

The day invents me
larger than life, human,
a curious condition. And
even more curious, my soul,
which I thought a frail thing,
demands job security, double pay
for overtime. Relax I say,
we are on holiday, enjoy the trip
through the San Juan Islands,

the sun in a white heat
lusting after sailboats, cabin cruisers,
passengers seated on the Elwha's deck
colourful as rows of flowers,
God's thoughts, Paz wrote.

Promenading, I avoid sooty streamers,
the old ferry's spent oil fumes,
lean over the rail, breathe in
God's breath, the ocean's lively scents.
I am girlish, slightly giddy,
a big F for freedom on my chest,
like a letter on a sophomore's sweater.

Sidney to Friday Harbor, Orcas,
then down to the car deck,
the men in orange know
what they are doing, having packed
us in like smoked oysters
we drive out smoothly at Anacortes,

the sun, pink in the face
touches trees, the road
stretching ahead,
an adventure.

Esquimalt Woods

An old dead tree
grayed, impassive
its stunted trunk
its few dwarfed limbs

clumsily broken.

No leaf nor bud
no bark, no sweet sap
for wild small creature
or human beast.

Could this be Emily's tree?

She liked to trot her dogs
tote her easel, canvas,
food, into the woods,
her pack lumped
solid as herself
and her God.

Emily* prayed with paint.
God spoke to her in colours,
solemnly. His tones sombre
greens and browns
in western forests.

Tall, slender pines
arch up and up, lean protectively,
a nave. Wrap round silent space
the larger bulk and silence
of the old dead thing.

Light must struggle—
still, it enters
in, penetrates the cave,
and stays.

The tree I say is victory.
Emily found the Infinite
in her secret innermost
place.

*Emily Carr, a Canadian painter, a contemporary of
the Group of Seven.*

Back In School

Young faces, young dreams,
mine, a tattered flag,
flying through halls
exultant with bodies and voices
to my harbour, the Seminar Room.

I recognize a classmate,
noticed her sculpted torso
backlit by tall windows.
Looped golden earrings
caught the light, emphasized
the column of her neck.

I thought a breeze stirred.
I thought it might have come
from ancient Greece,
an island tongued
by the turquoise sea
into poetry. Did it sigh
for Sappho's violet eyes?

The professor drops his briefcase
on the table, anchors
grey wild hair, forked grey beard
above wine velvet jacket.
In his fierce smile
the winds of poetry
waken, stretch.

Song of the Right Breast

Oh my sister
your place is stark
and I am desolate
without you there.
You cannot speak to me,
you cannot hear.

I have lost my balance.
Who will share
secrets,
the silly fears?

Growing up together
we answered each
for each.
You were always
by my side,
your silky flesh
identical to mine.
Leaning we might touch
and smile, thinking
we were beautiful.

Oh my sister my twin
the song we sang together
will haunt me
until I die.

Love Letters For The World

To the men

Signals spill red petals
on pillows of November mist,
orange and scarlet poppies drift across wet roads.

You carry sheaves of poppies in your arms,
their green leaves fill your hands.
Carmine poppies spring from your shoulders
are wings at your heels.

You name the many names of midnight
lay your emblems down
crimson blazes in the dark,
without fanfare, you bring on morning light.

You know the body is only that, yet more,
we cannot *see* love still it surrounds us.

In your light the spelling of the bones,
wild blood's syllables
are easily deciphered.

You, they read, are love letters for the world.

Remembrance Day, November 11, 1991

Moonchild

Midnight blue blanket
tucked under her chin
the moon sleeps

a tired child

her features soft
her halo
tipped sideways

Gulls

their calmness
long sure strokes
streaking light

across

the dawn's
dark lilac fields

About the Author

Born in Toronto, Ontario, **Luella Kerr** attended night classes at the University of Toronto and did post graduate work at York University. Granted her M.A. in 1978, she settled in Victoria, British Columbia. Fiction, poetry and a television drama have been produced by the Canadian Broadcasting Corportation. Short stories and poems have appeared in many Canadian literary journals and in magazines in Wales and England. She has read from her work across Canada and for Radio Bermuda. Her previous books include *A Breath of Earth* and *Light of Mourning*, both from **Ekstasis Editions.**

She lives with an inventor, has one son in New York, the other in Toronto and now has a new baby grandson. When not writing she likes to paint and has been exhibited throughout the province of British Columbia. *Dance in the Cage of My Bones* is her eighth book.